From Chili
to Chocolate

Written by Susan Brocker

Mexico

My name is Lucita. I live in Mexico City with my mother, who is a chef. In her restaurant, she creates hot, spicy meals with plenty of chilies. Do you know any other ingredients that are popular in Mexican food?

Contents

Look for the **Activity Zone!**
When you see this picture, you will find
an activity to try.

Plenty of Plants

Mexico is a large country with many different landscapes and climates. It has hot, dry deserts, snow-capped mountains, and steamy, tropical jungles. Each region has an amazing variety of plants and crops, so it's not surprising that Mexico is famous for many different kinds of food.

Mexican food differs from region to region. In some areas, it is hot and spicy; in others, it is rich and sweet. Corn, beans, chilies, and chocolate are a few of the many foods first discovered in this part of the world.

At this market in Zaachila, in southern Mexico, people can buy both locally grown foods and foods from other parts of the country.

U.S.A.

Wheat
Cotton

MEXICO

Oranges

Gulf of Mexico

Beans
Corn   Bananas
Sugar cane
★   Rice
Mexico City   Coffee

PACIFIC OCEAN

Each crop is grown in the
parts of Mexico where
the climate suits it best.

Trading Food

Explorers from Spain came to Mexico
in the early 1500s. They introduced
many new food plants, such as wheat,
rice, and sugar cane.

The explorers took back to Europe
many native Mexican food plants, such
as chilies, corn, and cacao-bean trees,
from which chocolate is made.
Europeans had never tasted these
foods before.

introduce   to bring in a plant and grow
it in a new place

5

Corn Country

Corn is the staple food of Mexico. More farmers in Mexico grow corn than any other crop. Corn grows quickly and produces a large seedhead called a *cob*. It is ripe for harvesting when the seeds, or kernels, have swollen.

Many Mexicans use corn to make a round, flat bread called a *tortilla*. They grind the corn and mix it with water to form dough, which they roll flat and fry on a griddle. *Tortillas* are the basis of most Mexican meals. They are eaten plain or filled with a mixture of beans, meats, vegetables, and cheese.

staple   a food that is eaten most days and is an important part of a person's diet

Hundreds of years ago, popcorn was an important food for the Aztec people, who lived in Mexico. They also used it to make necklaces and headdresses for special ceremonies.

A Variety of Uses

Thousands of years ago, native Mexicans began growing corn. Today, many different kinds of corn are grown, and they all have different uses.

- Flour corn is the main corn grown in Mexico. Its kernels are soft and colorful.

- Sweet corn is the sweetest and is often eaten on the cob.

- Popcorn has a tough outer coat. Heating causes a popcorn grain to swell and the coat to explode and "pop."

- Dent corn has kernels that are dented at the tip. Farmers feed it to their animals.

- Waxy corn is starchy and used to thicken processed foods.

Corn is the third most important crop in the world, after rice and wheat. These crops are all a kind of food called *carbohydrates*, which provide the body with energy.

Basic Beans

Beans are another important food crop grown in Mexico. Many Mexicans do not eat much meat, and beans are a healthy substitute. They are easy to grow and are a rich source of protein and vitamins.

Mexicans usually boil, mash, and then fry and refry their beans, or *frijoles*. They have many types of beans to choose from in a variety of flavors, colors, and sizes. Choice and preparation depend on regional taste and tradition. White, pink, and mottled pinto beans are popular in the north, while in the south, red kidney beans and black beans are favorites.

Black beans

Pinto beans

Kidney beans

protein   a substance in food that helps build muscle and bone

1

Sprout Some Beans!

2

3

1. Rinse a handful of dried mung beans; then put them in a jar and cover them with water. Place a square of muslin over the top and fasten it with a rubber band. Place the jar in a warm, dark place.

2. The next day, pour the water out and rinse the swollen beans. Drain the beans well so that they are damp but not sitting in water. Place the jar back in the warm, dark place.

3. Rinse your beans twice a day. Keep them damp but not wet. The beans should sprout in two or three days. After about five days, gently transfer them to a strainer and rinse them under a faucet. You can now eat your sprouts in salads, sandwiches, or stir-fries.

A bean plant produces flowers. Insects fertilize each flower, and then part of the flower grows into a long, thin fruit called a *pod*. Inside the pod is a row of edible seeds, or beans.

fruit the part of a plant that contains the seeds; it can be a berry, a pod, or a nut

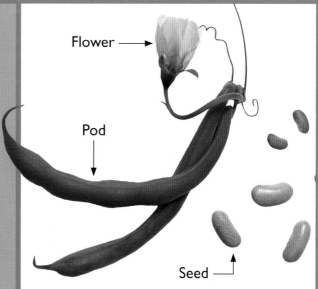

Flower →

Pod

Seed

Hot Chilies

Mexico is the home of chilies. More than one hundred varieties of chili peppers grow there. Since ancient times, Mexicans have used chilies to spice up their food. However, not all chilies are hot. Some taste sweet, and others are quite mild. Like beans, peppers are the fruit of a shrubby plant. However, unlike beans, we usually eat the fleshy outer wall of the pepper seed pod and discard the seeds.

Chilies are eaten fresh, dried, roasted, pickled, and ground. Mexicans often mix chilies with tomatoes, onions, and spices to make *salsa*, a spicy sauce.

These chilies are drying in the sun. This will preserve them so that they can still be used weeks or months later.

Seed pod (fruit) — Seeds

The Scoville Chart

In 1912, a chemist named Wilbur Scoville developed a method for rating the heat level of different kinds of chilies by measuring the amount of capsaicin in the fruit.

Rating	Chili Variety	Scoville Units
0	Pimento	0
1	New Mexican	100–1,000
2	Española	1,000–1,500
3	Sandia	1,500–2,500
4	Jalapeño	2,500–5,000
5	Serrano	5,000–15,000
6	Chile de Arbol	15,000–30,000
7	Cayenne	30,000–50,000
8	Santaka	50,000–100,000
9	Habanero	100,000–350,000
10	Tezpur	350,000–855,000

How hot a chili is depends on the amount of a chemical called *capsaicin* in the fruit. Capsaicin causes a burning sensation on the skin inside the mouth.

Sweet Treats

Some of the world's most tempting foods originated in Mexico. Chocolate is made from the seeds of the cacao tree, which grows in the tropical south. This tree produces large, melon-shaped pods. Each pod contains 20 to 40 seeds, or cacao beans.

Chocolate has a bitter taste unless it is sweetened. Mexicans like drinking frothy hot chocolate sweetened with vanilla. The fragrant essence of vanilla also comes from the Mexican tropics. It is made from the scented seed pods of the vanilla orchid.

Cacao plants grow in warm, wet places. Today, cacao plants are grown in Brazil and Africa as well as Mexico. When the pods are ripe, they are harvested, and the beans are removed from inside.

The vanilla plant is a tropical climbing orchid. The ancient Aztecs used vanilla in a drink called *xocoatl* (SHOK oh la till), which was made of ground cacao beans sweetened with vanilla and honey. Only royalty and warriors were allowed to drink it.

Making Chocolate

Chocolate is made by roasting dried cacao beans. The beans are then cracked and removed from their shells. Shelled beans are called *nibs*. The nibs are ground into pieces. The grinding heats the fat, or cocoa butter, in the beans into a liquid. The liquid and finely ground nibs are mixed to form chocolate liquor. This liquor forms the basis of all chocolate products.

A traditional Mexican sauce called *mole* is made from chocolate, chili peppers, and spices.

Fabulous Fruits

Many kinds of fruits grow in Mexico. Citrus fruits, such as oranges and lemons, grow in the cooler regions, while tropical fruits, such as papayas and pineapples, flourish in the hotter, wetter areas.

Fruits native to Mexico include the avocado, papaya, and guava. Avocados have been a vital part of the Mexican diet for centuries. They contain healthy fats and many nutrients. Mexicans eat them in a mildly spicy sauce called *guacamole*, which is a mix of mashed avocado with chilies, tomatoes, onions, and other flavorings. When the Spaniards arrived, they introduced tropical fruits from distant lands. Bananas came from Asia and Africa, pineapples from South America, and mangoes from India.

Avocado pickers harvest avocados when the skins are green. Later, some avocados ripen to a dark purple color. Sometimes, they are placed in cold storage to keep them from ripening too soon.

Today, many of the bananas grown in Mexico are exported to the United States.

export to sell something to another country

Fruit or Vegetable?

Avocados grow on trees and have a single large seed, or stone, surrounded by thick, green flesh. Many people think of avocados as a vegetable, but scientifically speaking, they are fruit. Fruits are the fleshy, seed-bearing parts of a plant, whereas vegetables are the edible leaves, stems, or roots of a plant.

Avocados

Flesh

Sliced flesh, ready to eat

Seed

Coffee and Cane

Coffee and sugar cane are two of Mexico's major export crops. Both products were introduced from other countries and flourish in the warm regions of Mexico.

The coffee plant is native to Africa. Coffee beans are the seeds of the coffee plant. Two beans grow inside each fruit, or berry. Sugar cane is a species of tall, tropical grass first cultivated in the South Pacific. The long, thick stalks contain a sugary sap, which is the source of most of the world's sugar.

A woman picks coffee beans.

cultivate   to grow and care for a particular plant

Sugar from Cane

Before coffee was a drink, people in Ethiopia made cakes from coffee berries to keep awake and alert. Coffee contains *caffeine*, a chemical that stimulates, or boosts, the nervous system.

1. Harvested canes are washed, shredded, and placed in a crushing machine, which squeezes the juice from the stalks.

2. The juice is heated with a mixture of lime and water to purify it.

3. The liquid is filtered and put in a tank, where most of the water dries off.

4. The leftover sugary syrup is heated in a vacuum pan to remove more water.

5. The syrup is put into a drum called a *centrifuge*, which spins rapidly and separates out the syrup, leaving behind crystals of raw sugar.

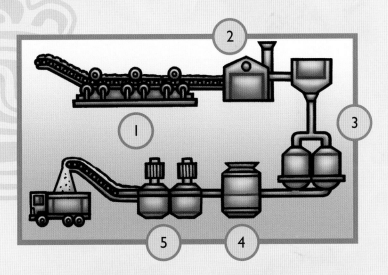

Sugar cane grows as high as 30 feet. In Mexico, workers cut down the cane using machetes, large knives with a special blade for cutting vegetation.

Desert Delights

The hot, dry deserts of northern Mexico are home to the world's greatest variety of cactuses and other water-storing, or succulent, plants. Long ago, native Mexicans discovered how to use these spiny plants as a source of food and drink.

Mexicans eat the fruit of many cactuses or grind the seeds into meal for cakes. They strip the spines off the fleshy pads of the prickly pear cactus and fry or pickle the pads. They roast the buds of the yucca plant to make candy and use the sap of the agave plant in drinks.

Waxy skin stops water from evaporating.

Thick, fleshy stems store water.

Roots grow near the surface to collect as much water as possible.

The fruits of the prickly pear cactus are called *tunas*. Tiny, irritating barbs cover the fruit, which must be peeled carefully before eating.

Cactus Smuggling

Wild cactus plants are sometimes dug up from Mexican deserts for sale to international collectors or garden landscapers. This trade is threatening many rare species. Some cactuses are now banned from trade, and others cannot be bought without an import permit. Gardeners can help save rare cactuses by buying them only from genuine nurseries that grow cactus plants from seed.

Spines and fine hairs protect the plant from grazing animals.

Ribs give the plant shade.

The cactus has adapted so that it can survive in the hot, dry desert.

import   to buy something from another country

Forests Forever

Forests cover nearly a fifth of Mexico. Pine and cedar forests grow in the cooler mountain regions, and lush, tropical rainforests grow in the south. Loggers cut down the pines to make paper and paper products. They also cut down the hardwood trees, such as ebony and mahogany, that grow in the rainforests. These trees are used to make furniture.

Vast tracts of rainforest are also cleared to make way for crops and cattle ranching. Many people are concerned that this is threatening the wide variety of Mexico's plant and animal life—its biodiversity. They believe that farming techniques must change in order for the forests to survive.

Plant biologist Mark Olson searches for rare plant species in Mexico. Many of the plants that grow there are found nowhere else on Earth. Mark is concerned that deforestation is destroying the places where they grow, and they could be lost to the world forever.

Wood from cone-bearing trees, such as pines, is called *softwood*. *Hardwood* comes from flowering, broadleaf trees, such as oak. Hardwood is generally stronger than softwood, but hardwood trees grow much more slowly than softwood trees and therefore take longer to replace.

| Pine | Oak |

Forest Farmers

Some Mexican farmers are starting to use forests in ways that will conserve them for the future. This is called *sustainable forestry*.

- Some loggers cut down trees on a rotational basis. This allows each area time to regrow.

- Instead of clearing forests, some farmers grow their crops under existing forest trees. The trees provide shade and prevent soil erosion, and their rotting leaves are a natural fertilizer.

- Farmers plant crops, such as beans, that put nutrients back into the soil.

A Colorful Country

For thousands of years, Mexicans have used plants
for all kinds of practical purposes as well as for food.
Today, many villagers dress in handwoven clothes
made from brightly colored cotton—a plant that grows
in some parts of Mexico. They use fruits, flowers,
leaves, and bark to make natural dyes to color the cloth.
Each region has its own distinctive patterns and designs.
The long, thin leaves of the agave plant are harvested to
produce sisal, a coarse fiber that is made into sandals,
ropes, mats, and hammocks.

A cotton seedpod is called a *boll*. When a boll dries, it bursts open to release its seeds, which are surrounded by a mass of cotton fibers.

Workers dry the long, thin fibers from agave leaves to make them into sisal.

Brightly painted puppets, masks, and dolls are made out of papier-mâché, grasses, straw, and wood.

Mexicans paint colorful *amate* paintings on the bark of fig and mulberry trees.

Find Out More!

1. Many Mexican foods come from the seeds or fruits of plants. Why do plants produce fruits, and how are they related to flowers?

2. Which parts of plants do the foods you eat come from?

To find out more about the ideas in *From Chili to Chocolate*, visit **www.researchit.org** on the web.

Index